Henrietta Louisa Lear

A Lenten Cookery Book

Being Nearly 200 Maigre Recipes

Henrietta Louisa Lear

A Lenten Cookery Book
Being Nearly 200 Maigre Recipes

ISBN/EAN: 9783744789028

Printed in Europe, USA, Canada, Australia, Japan

Cover: Foto ©Lupo / pixelio.de

More available books at **www.hansebooks.com**

A LENTEN

COOKERY BOOK,

BEING NEARLY

200 MAIGRE RECIPES.

EDITED BY

MRS. SIDNEY LEAR.

A. R. MOWBRAY & CO.,
LONDON : 25, WARWICK LANE, PATERNOSTER ROW.
OXFORD : 116, S. ALDATE'S STREET.

CONTENTS.

A LENTEN COOKERY BOOK.

HESE recipes have been gathered to-gether from various sources, most of them being brought from the Continent, and it has been thought by several people that they would prove useful if gathered together in a little book of specially Maigre Cookery. It will be obvious that much greater variety may be obtained by just combinations from the recipes here given ; and it seems to be a received opinion at the present time that variety in food is desirable on the score of wholesomeness as well as of agreeableness. It is hoped that this little collection may find its use in kitchens where a greater change of dishes made from simple materials is desired during seasons of abstinence.

One of the most useful forms of Maigre Cookery, and the least understood in England, is that of Soup. There is a great variety of this dish within easy reach of all who will take the trouble to prepare their materials. But as other soups depend mainly upon the stock which forms their foundation, so most vegetable soups depend very much upon being made with proper stock.

Most French Soups of this kind are founded on one of other of the following Maigre Stocks.

I.—Common Maigre Stock for Soups and Sauces.

Take 2 or 3℔s. of dry peas, (the hard kind,) wash, and boil them, adding water so as to prevent the peas from becoming cooked, (a bit of iron, such as a key, in the pot will prevent their softening). Let them boil for some hours, and use the broth, filling the pot up with cold water as you do so. Then take plenty of carrots and onions; cut the first in pieces, and the onions across. Pass them in a stewpan with butter till they are half-browned, then cover them with some bits of parsley *roots*, leeks, mushrooms, sprigs of parsley, and small white onions whole, a very little thyme and mint, a bay leaf, a carp's body, (keeping the flesh for stuffing). Moisten with a little hot water, and let it simmer over a slow fire. In an hour add more hot water, and make a hotter fire. Then take the pot by both handles and shake it constantly till the contents are coloured, but not burnt or blackened. Then mix the purée of peas, which ought to be clear ; boil gently for an hour or two ; pass through a tammy, and clear carefully of all grease.

II.—Fish Stock for Soups and Sauces

Prepare a clear purée of split peas, as before. Then take the remains of any kind of fish, salt or freshwater ; put them in a stewpan, with an onion with one or two cloves stuck into it, some slices of carrot, and a bouquet of herbs, salt and pepper ; moisten with half water and half purée, add a piece of bread crumb, and a bit of butter. Cook well and strain.

This stock is a good foundation for almost all maigre soups. The addition of some crab shells grated or well crushed boiled in it, and then (after straining through a cloth) rather highly seasoned, will make a good *bisque d'écrevisses*, to which no further addition is needed, save some croutons fried.

Again what the French call " Roux," which is sometimes called " brown butter " in England, is constantly required in cooking maigre dishes. It simply consists of

III.

Two ounces of butter, slowly melted in a pan : add 3 oz. of flour, and stir with a wooden spoon till it becomes of a golden brown. This is added to colour soups and sauces.

IV.

What is called a *liaison* consists of the yolk of two eggs mixed with six or eight tablespoonfuls of milk or cream, passed through a sieve, and used to unite other sauces.

V.

Brown thickening for sauces is made by melting a pound of butter over a slow fire, and carefully taking off the scum. Then pour the butter into another stewpan ; add a pound of sifted flour, mix well with a wooden spoon, and stir over the fire till it is of a light brown colour. Put into an earthenware pan, and use as required.

VI.

White thickening is made in the same way, only

in order to prevent browning the mixture, the fire must be kept very slow while baking.

VII.

Fried bread crumbs are prepared by putting, say 4 oz. of very stale, fine crumbs into a frying-pan, with an ounce of butter, stir with a spoon till they are light brown. Then put the crumbs on a sheet of paper to clear off the grease, and keep till wanted.

VIII.—Fish Forcemeat.

The fish (of whatever kind) must be carefully cleared of bones, and put through a wire sieve. Then mix with butter, in the proportion of one half the weight of fish, and the same of bread panada (No. IX). Pound these together, adding two or three eggs, and seasoning.

IX.—Bread Panada.

Steep 1 ℔. of crumb of bread in lukewarm water ; wring it in a cloth. Put in a stewpan with 1 oz. of butter and a little salt, and stir over the fire till it is a firm, smooth paste. Let it cool before mixing with other materials.

This is a necessary foundation for all stuffing or forcemeat.

X.—Frying Batter.

To three quarters of a pound of flour add 2 oz. of melted butter, and two yolks of egg; mix with a wooden spoon, pouring in about three quarters of a pint of warm water, and work with the spoon till it be like smooth cream. It must stand awhile before used, and just before use three whites of egg whipped into froth must be stirred lightly in.

XI.—Bechamel Sauce.

Chop two shalots, some parsley, and small onions not very finely, into fresh butter. Moisten with cream or milk, and boil till the mixture is reduced to half. Season with a little salt, pass through a tammy into another saucepan, add some nutmeg and a little bit of butter rolled in flour. Stir this sauce over the fire till it is smooth, and serve.

XII.—Cream Bechamel Sauce.
(French recipe.)

Take 2 oz. of butter and 4 oz. of flour; work them together with a wooden spoon; put into a saucepan with a chopped onion, a carrot, a bit of celery, sprig of parsley, a bay leaf, a sprig of thyme, pepper, salt, and nutmeg; moisten with a pint of milk; stir over the fire, and let it boil; strain into a basin. When wanted put some of this sauce into a saucepan with a few sliced mushrooms, and while on the fire stir in cream in proportion of one half of the whole quantity.

XIII.—Sauce Piquante.

Slice some onions, a few mushrooms, carrots, turnips, and parsley roots, into melted butter; sprinkle with a little flour; moisten with any wine and maigre stock in equal parts; season with salt and spice. Add a handful of roughly-chopped shalots, a head of garlic, a tarragon leaf, a bay leaf, and a sprig of basil thyme. Boil for a good quarter of an hour, pass through a tammy, and skim off all grease. Then add a few whole capers, two pickled gherkins chopped, and (if agreeable) one or two anchovies well cleaned and chopped small. Warm the sauce without letting it boil. It may be served with slices of lemon.

XIV.—Dutch Sauce.

Four yolks of egg to 2 oz. of butter, a tablespoonful of cream, a teaspoonful of elder, chili, or tarragon vinegar, with pepper, salt, and nutmeg. The pan in which these are should be put into a saucepan of hot water over the fire, and the mixture be stirred quickly with a wooden spoon till it becomes like cream.

XV.—Celery Sauce.

Slice three or four heads of celery small, and stew very gently with a sliced onion ; 3 or 4 oz of butter, and seasoning. Do not let the celery brown, and when soft, add 3 oz. of flour, and a pint of milk. Stir and boil for above twenty minutes, pass through a tammy. It must be heated again for use.

XVI.—Italian Sauce.

Take a dessert spoonful of salad oil, and the same quantity of chopped shalots mixed with a little thyme or other herbs. Stir till the shalots are lightly fried (not coloured). Add a tablespoonful of chopped mushrooms, half a pint of maigre stock, a little "*roux*" or brown butter, and a little white wine. Boil and skim.

XVII.—Maître d'Hôtel Sauce.

Heat some Bechamel Sauce, stir in a piece of butter, (about 2 oz. to a gill of sauce,) a tablespoonful of chopped parsley, and lemon juice to taste.

XVIII.—Sharp Maître d'Hôtel Sauce.

To the above sauce add a tablespoonful of Tarragon vinegar, the same of chili vinegar, and a teaspoonful of anchovy, or of lemon juice, boiled separately for a few minutes.

XIX.—Geneva Sauce.

Chop half-a-dozen good sized mushrooms, with a few shalots, and a little parsley. Put them into a stewpan with a piece of butter, and stir over the fire for five minutes; then add a gill of maigre stock, a spoonful of flour, pepper, salt, and nutmeg, a tablespoonful of lemon juice, and a little sugar, and boil.

XX.—Gooseberry Sauce.

Boil half-a-pint of green gooseberries, drain and rub through a hair sieve. Stew with a tablespoonful of chopped sorrel or spinage; add a bit of butter, and pepper, salt, and sugar. Serve with fish.

XXI.—Mustard Sauce.

Melt the quantity of butter required, and then stir in a teaspoonful (or less) of mustard, with a dessert spoonful of chili vinegar. You may add some fish roe, or anchovy, or chopped sardine, if agreeable.

XXII.—Indian Sauce.

To half-a-pint of Tomata Sauce (No. XXIX.) add a dessert spoonful of curry powder, a teaspoonful of chili vinegar, and boil.

XXIII.—Red Sauce.

To half-a-pint of stock, add 2 oz. of currant jelly, a glass of red wine, and a few peppercorns. Boil for five minutes.

XXIV.—Mayonnaise Sauce.

Take three yolks of eggs, with pepper and salt, and work them in a basin with a wooden spoon into half-a-pint of olive oil and a tablespoonful of Tarragon vinegar, till the mixture is like thick cream.

This sauce is always eaten cold, with fish, fish or other salads, &c.

XXV.—Wine Sauce.

To a glass of wine add a tablespoonful of lemon juice, three chopped shalots, a little cayenne pepper, and a tablespoonful of any sauce, according to the flavour you desire,—Harvey, Worcester, Tarragon vinegar, &c. Boil for five minutes, and strain.

XXVI.—The same, as Sweet Sauce.

Instead of the shalots add chopped citron peel, a bit of cinnamon instead of cayenne, and any syrup,—orange, currant, cherry, &c.,—instead of the sauce.

XXVII.—Mushroom Sauce.

To twelve tablespoonfuls of stock add six or eight chopped mushrooms ; boil with sugar and peppercorns, or cayenne.

XXVIII.—Shalot Sauce.

A tablespoonful of chopped shalot, two of vinegar, spice.   Boil; then add ten tablespoonfuls of stock and a little sugar.

XXIX.—Tomata Sauce.

Boil six sliced shalots, with herbs and a wine-glass of vinegar, for five minutes; then add six bruised tomatas, and some sugar.   Stir and boil for five minutes; pass through a coarse strainer.

Crosse and Blackwell's preserved tomata pulp can safely be used instead of fresh tomatas.   A $\frac{1}{4}$lb. to six tomatas.

XXX.—White Sauce.

Boil a quarter of a pint of milk with an onion and some seasoning; when boiling stir in an ounce of flour and two of butter, ready mixed.   Stir till quite smooth.   Strain; mix two yolks of eggs with a little cream, and stir into the first mixture over the fire, without allowing it to boil.

XXXI.—Egg Sauce.

Take any White Sauce, and when hot stir slowly in two or three hard boiled eggs chopped small, not minced.

XXXII.—Curry.

Slice six large onions, and stew over a slow fire in 2 oz. of butter. Add two sliced apples, and stew till these are mixed; then add a tablespoonful of curry powder, a teaspoonful of vinegar, two of flour, some salt and sugar. Moisten with a quart of maigre stock, or milk, or water, or either of these mixed. Boil till it is thick, and strain through a tammy.

XXXIII.—Purée of Dried Peas.

Take the largest size of split peas, wash in hot water, boil in cold, adding water as the peas absorb it. When they are thoroughly done strain through a sieve.

XXXIV.—Pea Soup.

A quart of split peas, two onions, a carrot, and a head of celery, (chopped,) to three quarts of water. Simmer three or four hours over the fire, occasionally adding a little water; pass through a sieve, and boil again, adding one ounce of butter, pepper and salt.

Serve with dried powdered mint, and dice of fried bread.

XXXV.—Bourgeoise Soup.

Scrape or peel lightly four turnips, if large cut them ; pluck four leeks, and cut into inch long pieces and wash them. The same with some bits of celery. Pluck and cut four onions ; stew all in a small pot, with water, salt, and a little butter. (You may fry the turnips first if you think proper.) When these vegetables are thoroughly done, take a purée of dried peas, add the vegetables and some pepper, boil altogether, season to taste, and serve.

XXXVI.—White Turnip Soup.

Scrape and peel and cut up turnips according to the quantity of soup required, and put them to boil in lukewarm water. When half done, add one fifth as much of onion cut up, pepper and salt. When thoroughly done, take off the fire, and add a cup of milk and a piece of butter, stir well, and serve with dice of fried bread.

XXXVII.—Onion Soup.

Cut six large onions into slices, and put them

into a stewpan with butter until they are brown ; moisten with a little hot water, and stew ; then add two quarts of maigre stock (of purée of peas) ; add black pepper and salt, and boil the whole up several times.

XXXVIII.—Belgian Turnip Soup.

Two pound of turnips cut into dice, 4 oz. butter, two chopped onions, a dessert spoonful of brown sugar, pepper and salt, to two quarts of water. Simmer for twenty minutes, stir in a cupful of flour and a quart of milk ; boil for twenty minutes, and serve with dice of fried bread.

XXXIX.—Cabbage Soup (White).

Chop some cabbages, and put into a pot with onions cut in quarters, 2 oz. of butter, salt and peppercorns, and boil slowly in water; when thoroughly cooked add milk according to taste.

XL.—Brown Cabbage Soup.

Stew the chopped cabbages in water with pepper and salt ; pass some sliced onions in another stewpan with brown butter, and when the onions are browned moisten them with a little stock, pour over the cabbage and boil.

XLI.—Dutch Cabbage Soup.

Butter a tureen and sprinkle it with cheese; put in a layer of cabbage sprinkled with cheese, and another of bread crumb also sprinkled; then cabbage again, and bread, always letting the uppermost be cabbage. Pour a little stock over the whole; put the tureen for a short time into the oven, and serve.

XLII.—Chesnut Soup.

Shell, scald, and scrape two score chesnuts; boil them slowly in a pint of milk, drain and rub through a wire sieve; put into a stewpan with an ounce of butter, a teaspoonful of sugar, a little cream, pepper and salt; stir till well mixed, and then stir in a pint of milk and a pint of stock, till just boiling.

XLIII.—Carrot Soup.

Scrape a dozen carrots, parboil, drain, and put them into a stewpan with a pint of milk, two onions, some chopped celery, 2 oz. of butter, and seasoning. Let this simmer till the carrots are quite soft;

beat up well, add two pints of stock and a little sugar, and heat just short of boiling.

XLIV.—French Soupe aux Choux.

Three pounds of white cabbage cut in strips, to a gallon of water, and 2 oz. of butter, two large onions, a carrot, turnip, head of celery, and any other available green vegetable, such as leek, peas, or some sliced lettuce. Boil for a couple of hours, season with black pepper, salt, and a little brown sugar. Cover the bottom of the soup tureen with stale bread, leaving the crust on; pour the soup over it, and cover all up closely by the fire for a few minutes, to let the bread get well soaked, and serve.

XLV.—Lentil or Dried Haricot Soup.

Slice three or four onions, a turnip, and carrot, into a stewpan, with a quarter of a pound of butter, some parsley, thyme, and a bay leaf; stir till these are getting brown; then add a quart of lentils or haricots and three quarts of water, or maigre stock; let all simmer till the lentils are soft; then season with salt and sugar, and serve either as it is or strained through a tammy.

C

XLVI.—Soupe a la Paysanne.

Put a pint of peas into four quarts of water, and
when they begin to boil, add them to another pot
in which two or three onions, carrots, turnips, some
celery, and any herbs, leeks, &c., have been lightly
browned in a quarter of a pound of butter. Boil
both together, throwing in some crusts of bread,
pepper, and salt ; then let the whole simmer for an
hour or two. When about to serve, sprinkle some
finely chopped leek or shalot on the top.

XLVII.—Bourgeois Soup Maigre.

Four carrots, two leeks, one turnip, two large
onions, two large potatoes, a handful of dried peas.
Put together in a soup pot with four quarts of cold
water ; boil four hours, pass through a sieve ; add
a piece of butter, pepper and salt, a little more
water. Boil for half-an-hour and serve, adding
a little boiled rice or sliced potato.

XLVIII.—Soupe de Strasbourg.

Chop four or five lettuces, a cucumber, one or
two onions, a little chervil, parsley, and a leaf or
two of tarragon, into a pot with an ounce of butter,

nutmeg, salt, and pepper, and a little sugar ; simmer
for a quarter of an hour, then add a good spoonful
of flour; mix with three pints of maigre stock ; stir
till it boils ; then let it simmer gently, and just
before serving stir in half-a-pint of cream, six yolks
of eggs, and some sugar.

This soup may be more economically made by
using a pint of milk instead of cream, diminishing
the quantity of stock accordingly.

XLIX.—Celery Soup.

Slice six heads of celery with four or five onions
into 4 oz. of butter and a pint of maigre stock.
Simmer till soft; then add ½℔. of flour, pepper and
salt, mix well.   Add a quart more either of stock
or milk, and stir over the fire for a quarter of
an hour ; pass through a tammy, and heat.   (Add
a half-pint of cream if made without milk.)   Serve
with fried croutons.

L.—Vegetable Marrow Soup.

Take the core out of two or more marrows,
(according to size,) put in a stewpan with 2 oz.
of butter, a chopped onion, nutmeg, pepper, salt,

and sugar, and a pint of water. Boil gently, pass through a tammy ; add a pint of Maigre Stock, and a pint of milk, or half-pint of cream. Stir well over the fire, and serve with fried croutons.

LI.—Common Vegetable Soup.

Strip and wash any vegetables, such as lettuce, sorrel, spinage, chervil, leeks, French beans, &c. Chop them slightly, and stew them with a bit of butter over a slow fire, often turning them with a wooden spoon, and when thoroughly done mix a little flour. Then add water, boil for a minute ; add a *liasion* (see No. 4) of yolk of egg, and pour over thin slices of bread, putting the vegetables in last so that they may float at the top.

LII.—Potato Soup.

Take five or six mealy potatoes, and cut them into small slices with an onion and a little bit of celery. Boil in three pints of water till all is tender; pass through a sieve. Boil again with a bit of butter, pepper, salt, and sugar, and just before serving stir in two tablespoonfuls of cream. The cream must be added *after* the last boiling.

LIII.—Brittany Potato Soup.

Take potatoes and half as many onions (say twelve and six), boil in a quart of water till quite in pulp. Rub through a sieve; add about 2 or 3 oz. of butter, pepper, salt, and sugar, and a few chopped mushrooms, and heat (not boil) with two quarts of milk.

LIV.—Paris Potato Soup.

Slice a dozen potatoes and half as many onions into a stewpan with 4 oz. of butter, nutmeg, sugar, pepper and salt. Add two quarts of maigre stock, and boil gently over a slow fire. Pass through a tammy; stir in half-a-pint of cream, and a few button mushrooms. Stir over the fire till quite hot, and serve with fried croutons.

This soup is sometimes made without the mushrooms, stirring in a few fresh green peas, or chopped French beans, or chopped gherkins, according to the season, with a few dice of fried bread.

LV.—Herring Broth.

Chop four turnips, two carrots, two onions, a

lettuce, some parsley and herbs, with a herring. Boil in four quarts of water slowly for three hours. Season and serve very hot, either with all or part of the vegetables left in according to taste.

LVI.—Oyster Soup.

Scald, drain, and wash two dozen oysters; nearly melt 2 oz. of butter, mix 2 oz. of flour with it, add a pint of fish stock; put in a small tea-spoonful of anchovy, a little nutmeg, and a tea-spoonful of chili vinegar. Add a quarter of a pint of cream, and stir over the fire till it boils gently. Cut up the oysters, put them into the tureen, and pour the soup over them..

LVII.—Soupe a la Mer.

Take the liquor in which any sea fish has been boiled, add sliced onions and carrots, a small bay-leaf, some parsley, and a scrap of garlic. Put it in a pot on the fire, and when at boiling point throw in some lettuce hearts, chervil, a stick of celery, and some sorrel, slightly chopped; when these are cooked add a *liaison* of yolk of eggs, season, and pour on to slices of bread in the bottom of the tureen.

This soup may also be made boiling the fish with the vegetables, keeping the fish in it, and passing the whole through a tammy before the second boiling, when the lettuce, &c., is added.

LVIII.—Lobster Soup.

Chop up an onion, carrot, some shalots, parsley, thyme, celery, and a bay-leaf; pass in a stewpan with butter till just browned, mix in 4 oz. of flour. Then stir into two or three pints of fish stock (see page 3), or water. After boiling, let it simmer awhile; then put in a cooked lobster from which the best part of the tail and claws has been removed, and which has been bruised in a mortar, and boil. Pass through a tammy, and skim; add a very little white wine, a spoonful of lemon juice, a teaspoonful of anchovy, pepper and salt. Put the meat from the tail and claws, cut small, into a tureen, and pour the soup hot upon it, and serve. Tinned lobster may be used for this. Crab soup may be made in the same way, with the addition of a little cream instead of wine.

LIX.—Rice Soup.

Half a pound of rice, stew for two hours in half

a gallon of water with a bit of butter, a mealy
potato, a turnip, carrot, onion, head of celery, two
or three Jerusalem artichokes, and a little parsley,
all cut into dice.   Then add a pint of maigre stock,
with pepper and salt, one or two cloves, a bay-leaf,
and a little thyme.   Boil up (and before serving
stir in a little cream and a few button mushrooms).

LX.—Macaroni Soup.

Soak 4 oz. of macaroni for two hours, throw
it into a pint of boiling milk and water ; add an
onion, some salt and pepper, and a tablespoonful
of stale bread crumbs.   Boil gently, pass through a
sieve ; put on the fire again, (not to boil,) and add
a gill of cream, (or milk,) a little bit of butter,
a few peppercorns, and a little nutmeg, and serve.

The same recipe may be used for vermicelli
soup.

LXI.—Barley Soup.

Boil a quarter of a pound of barley in one pint
of water ; add two pints of stock, while boiling ;
put in a chopped onion, 1 oz. of butter, a little
cinnamon, nutmeg, pepper and salt, and half-a-pint
of milk (or cream) ; stew for ten minutes, and

serve, either straining away the barley or not, according to taste.

LXII.—Sago Soup.

Steep ¼ ℔. of sago for some time in cold water ; put into a pot with two quarts of water or stock, an onion, turnip, some celery, a ¼ ℔. of stale bread, pepper corns, salt, and a little sugar ; when soft, rub through a sieve, and add a pint of boiling milk, serve with fried bread.

LXIII.—Vegetable Purée.

Cut up finely three large onions, three turnips, one carrot, and four or five potatoes; put into a stewpan with a quarter of a pound of butter (or half butter and half dripping), and a bunch of parsley and herbs ; pass over a brisk fire for ten minutes ; then add two tablespoonfuls of flour, stirring it in with two quarts of maigre stock and a pint of boiling milk ; season with salt, pepper, and sugar ; pass through a tammy, boil again, skim, and serve with fried croutons.

LXIV.—Kenn Soup.

Stew six Jerusalem artichokes and a large onion

in water till tender ; then add as much milk as will make up three pints in all, two yolks of egg, pepper and salt, and pass through a sieve.

(The ordinary ways of dressing fish, used on all occasions, are not inserted here, these being taken for granted. The following recipes are more such as are specially intended for maigre seasons as a variety.)

LXV.—Turbot au Gratin.

Pull the remains of cooked turbot and mix with some Bechamel sauce (No. 11); heat it in a stew-pan, and when placed in the dish, sprinkle it well with grated cheese, pour a little cream over it, and brown with a salamander.

LXVI.—Turbot or Sole en retraite.

Chop the cooked fish small with two hard boiled eggs, mix with stale bread crumbs half as much as the fish, moisten with a little cream or hot milk, add a few chopped gherkins, peppercorns, a little spice ; put all into a dish and cover with a layer, not more than an inch thick, of mashed potatoes, and brown it lightly ; or the fish may be surrounded with the potato, and left open at the top.

LXVII.—Fillets of Sole fried.

Flour the fillets, and dip them in well beaten egg, roll them in bread crumbs, and fry them lightly in butter, oil, or dripping ; serve with fried parsley.

These may be also served with almost any of the sauces given above.

LXVIII.—Fillets of Sole a la Cressy.

Take the ordinary fillets, keeping them flat instead of curling them, season with a little vinegar, pepper, salt, and sliced onion ; then dip lightly into frying butter, each fillet separately, turning them with a fork so that they may be evenly cooked. They will take about twenty minutes ; serve with tomata sauce. (No. 29).

LXIX.—Fillets of Sole au Champignons.

Bread crumb the soles and fry as usual, having some mushrooms chopped very fine, and sprinkle over the fillets as they are frying. When dished sprinkle lightly with bread crumbs browned ; then serve as they are, or with mushroom sauce.

LXX.—Sole au Gratin.

Split the sole, and take out the bones ; put an

ounce of butter into a stewpan, with various herbs
and a few mushrooms chopped together, and
seasoned with pepper, salt, nutmeg, and a little
vinegar. After this has been a few minutes on the
fire, put half the mixture into the sole ; then put it
on a buttered dish, spread the rest of the mixture
over it, sprinkle it with bread crumbs, and moisten
with a little white wine. and water; put a little
butter over the crumbs to brown them, and cook
in an oven or on a hot-plate. It should take from
a quarter of an hour to twenty minutes.

LXXI.—Carp en hachis.

Take some small fresh carp, bone them, and
mince the flesh with a few mushrooms, parsley, and
small white onions ; melt (about a quarter of the
weight of fish) butter in a stewpan, put in the
mince, stir it, moistening with a little white wine
and maigre stock ; season with salt, spice, and a
bunch of herbs ; cook over a slow fire, stirring
frequently. Serve on slices of toast, or in mashed
potato.

LXXII.—Carp (or other fish) a la Russe.

Sprinkle the fish with pepper and salt, put it

through some flour, and into a dish freely buttered, with one or more glasses of white wine, according to the size of the fish, and put into the oven or on a hot-plate. Prepare a bed of choucroute (pickled cabbage) stewed with butter; lay the fish on this, garnish with stewed mushrooms and sliced gherkins, and serve.

LXXIII.—Fish Toast.

Pound any remains of fish with a little butter, pepper, salt, chopped parsley, chopped onion, and enough cream to moisten it into a paste; heat it for a moment, spread on very hot toast, sprinkle with bread crumbs, and serve.

LXXIV.--Bouille-à-baisse.

This favourite Provençale dish is best made with a mixture of red mullet, mackerel, cod, sole, lobster, crab, and other such fish. These must be cut up, mixed with some chopped onion, and passed in butter (not browned) in a rather flat saucepan; then moisten the contents with olive oil, add an onion, a head of garlic, a bay leaf, some slices of lemon, one or two tomatas fresh or preserved, some salt, a pinch of saffron, and a glass of white wine; then add enough cold water to cover the fish entirely, and put on a quick fire. The fish should be cooked in quarter of an hour; then add a spoonful of chopped parsley, give it another half-boiling, and pour the liquid over slices of bread about half an inch thick, serving the fish in a separate dish garnished with the materials of their seasoning. The two dishes are to be taken together.

LXXV.—Bouille à baisse a la Marseillaise.

Put a saucepan of water on the fire containing some sliced onions, a bay leaf, head of garlic, some cloves, salt, and pepper. Cut off the heads of the fish about to be used, and boil them in this pan, then strain the liquor. Then put some olive oil and chopped onion in a larger stewpan on the fire, and put in the fish of all kinds cut up in slices; throw in parsley, some chopped garlic, some sliced lemon, and purée of tomata, salt, pepper, and a little powdered saffron; moisten with olive oil and white wine, then cover entirely with the liquor made above, and boil over a hot fire. Serve as in No. preceding.

LXXVI.—Fish Pudding.

Chop fine any fish already cooked, as much as will three parts fill a small pudding basin ; stew it for a short time with a little butter and pepper ; then take an ordinary French roll, or the same quantity of stale bread which has been soaked in milk for an hour, and beat it up well with the fish, add a few chopped gherkins (and mushrooms or truffles) and a couple of eggs ; beat all up well together, put into the oven, or boil, and serve with anchovy, Italian, or Geneva sauce.

LXXVII.—Pulled Fish.

Pull the remains of any cooked fish with a fork, put into a stewpan with a little butter, pepper, and salt, and a spoonful of cream ; when quite hot, dish, brown over with bread crumbs, and serve.

LXXVIII.—Kadgeree.

Take any fish (sole, haddock, or cod are best), and to two pounds of fish take a cupful of rice boiled well, and strained so as to be in separate grains, though soft; put the fish into a saucepan, add 2 oz. of butter, Cayenne pepper, and salt; when quite hot mix in the rice, and two hard-boiled eggs chopped small; mix well, and serve very hot.

LXXIX.—Fish Rissolles.

Take any cooked fish, and chop it fine, with the yolk of two hard-boiled eggs, about the same quantity of stale bread crumbs, an anchovy, a stick of boiled celery, spice, and salt. Pound all together with a little stock, and 2 oz. of butter, and two eggs beaten up. Make into balls, and fry lightly in bread crumbs.

LXXX.—Fish Sausages.

Pound some cooked fish, (lobster, or crab, or oysters the best,) and mix into a thick paste, with bread crumbs, yolk of egg (hard-boiled), parsley, herbs, and a few mushrooms. Divide the paste into pieces the size of a small sausage, and fry them in butter. Serve on mashed potato.

LXXXI.—Water Souché.

Take half-a-dozen flounders, perch, or other fresh-water fish; put them in a stewpan with half-a-pint of water, a little scraped horse-radish, seasoning, and a good handful of parsley ; stew for ten minutes or so ; put the fish into a small tureen, pour the liquor over very hot, and serve.

LXXX.—Normandy Pie.

Cut up potatoes, carrots, celery, and any vegetable except cabbage, into a pie-dish. Add a handful of well-soaked split peas, two hard-boiled eggs, a little chopped onion and parsley, and a bit of butter, pepper and salt. Moisten with stock or cream. Cover with a very light crust, and bake.

LXXXI.—Dutch Potato Pie.

Butter a flat dish, and put a layer of bread crumbs in. Then carefully break from four to six eggs into it ; lay some very thin slices of gherkin upon them. Then put a layer of nearly an inch thick of very light mashed potato over the whole. Sprinkle with bread crumbs, and put into the oven till the eggs are cooked, and the potato brown.

LXXXII.—Lausanne Egg Pie.

In the same way, put a layer of well-strained,

boiled rice into the dish ; pour enough curry sauce over to cover the rice. Then put a layer of thinly sliced potato (cooked), then two or three sardines, (these may be omitted according to taste). Then another layer of curry sauce. On that two or three hard-boiled eggs chopped, and finish with rice, sprinkled with bread crumbs.

LXXXV.—Omelette.

Break three eggs into a basin, add a spoonful of cream, and little piece of butter, pepper and salt. Take 2 oz. of butter in an omelette pan, and while it is melting, whip the eggs thoroughly ; when the butter begins to splutter, pour the eggs in and stir. As it becomes firm roll the omelette, let it brown on one side, and serve.

LXXXVI.—Omelette with Herbs.

The same as above, only put chopped parsley, shalot, thyme or tarragon, with the eggs before you beat them up.

LXXXVII.—Italian Omelette.

To four eggs, add 2 oz. of grated cheese, pepper and salt. Beat up together, and proceed the same as before.

LXXXVIII.—Potato Omelette.

To six eggs, add two tablespoonfuls of very light mashed potatoes. Beat up with cream, a little bit of butter, pepper and salt, and fry.

LXXXIX.—Onion Omelette.

Slice five or six young onions, and bake with a little butter, pepper and salt, till they are quite tender. Beat up four eggs, add a cupful of milk, a spoonful of cream, two tablespoonfuls of bread crumbs, and the onions. Bake in an ordinary pie-dish, and either serve in it, or turn it out, and add a sauce, Bechamel or other.

XC.—Fisherman's Omelette.

Take any small fish, or remains of other, chop them coarsely with an onion, a shalot, and a bit of garlic. Put into a saucepan with a tuft of herbs, add salt and pepper, and moisten with common red wine. Put on to a hot fire, boil for half-an-hour. Meanwhile, knead some butter and flour into eight or ten balls the size of a nut, and put them into a hot dish. Prepare eggs as usual, put them on the balls, pour the saucepan over them, roll a little, and serve.

XCI.—Eggs au Gratin.

Boil the eggs hard, shell and slice them. Put as much white sauce as will cover the slices into a stewpan, add some butter, some grated cheese, nutmeg, the yolk of two or more eggs, and a spoonful of lemon juice. Stir this over the fire till it is thick. Put the egg slices into a hot dish in layers, spreading this mixture between each; cover the top with it, sprinkle with fried bread crumbs and grated cheese, garnish with fried croutons. Put the whole into the oven for a few minutes, and serve.

XCII.—Egg Croquets.

Boil some eggs hard, chop them fine, beginning with the whites; pound them in a mortar with some finely-chopped parsley and leek, (or small white onions), salt, pepper, and nutmeg, and a little butter, carefully melted, and passed through a strainer. Mix and pound all together well; bind with one or two raw eggs, make into shape, dip into butter or egg and bread crumbs; fry of a light brown, and serve with fried parsley.

XCIII.—Fromage aux Œufs.

Weigh your eggs, and take a third of their weight in grated cheese, and a sixth of butter. Break the eggs into a stewpan, mix the cheese and butter, put more pepper than salt; while on the fire stir with a wooden spoon till the whole is thick and smooth. Turn out upon a hot dish, with or without hot toast beneath.

XCIV.—Swiss Omelette.

Have some peas ready stewed, let them get cold. Then prepare your omelette with a little cream. Mix the peas, and serve as usual.

The same may be done with asparagus tops, or French beans.

XCV.—Hard Eggs a l'Annecy.

Half-boil the eggs in boiling water; throw them into cold water; shell them, and cut them in half; take out the yolks, and chop them fine. Put some butter, with some chopped mushrooms, into a saucepan; soon add the yolks with some parsley, and a little chopped white onion. Stir all up with one or two raw eggs. Then stuff the white halves, and serve them either in white sauce, or a bed of spinach.

XCVI.—Eggs au beurre noir.

Break the eggs carefully into a dish; season them with pepper and salt. Have ready a frying-pan with butter, and when the butter leaves off spluttering, slip the eggs gently into it; when nearly done, pass a red hot iron over them to cook the yolks. Dish the eggs; pour a little vinegar nto the butter left in the frying-pan, heat it for a moment, pour over the eggs, and serve.

XCVII.—Billiard Eggs.

Half a pound of bread crumbs, mixed with 2 oz. of butter, a chopped onion, some herbs, and, if convenient, a sliced truffle; season to taste. Beat two or three eggs well in a little milk. Add two tablespoonfuls of cream. Roll into balls, and fry in egg and bread crumb. Serve with potato balls fried in the same manner, alternately.

XCVIII.—Genoese Eggs.

Two or three hard-boiled eggs, chopped very small; mix thoroughly with two or three table-spoonfuls of rice, boiled well, but each grain dry and separate. Put into a stewpan with a bit of butter, a little flour, and some chopped parsley, salt and pepper. When quite hot, put on to slices of toast, in a heap, and serve with a small slice of lemon on the top of each.

XCIX.—Eggs en pâté.

Boil some eggs, not quite hard, shell, dredge with black pepper, dipping the egg first into cream, or lightly buttering it. Then wrap it up in a very thin, light, puff paste, and bake.

C.—Eggs en Marinade.

Prepare as before, but instead of puff paste, put the eggs into a light batter, and fry them.

CI.—Egg Fritters.

Cut each (half-boiled) egg in two; take out the yolk, and chop it up, with a bit of sardine, and a little pepper. Fill up the whites with this, put into batter, and fry.

CII.—Eggs à la Campagnarde.

Take four or six eggs, according to what is wanted, beat them well, and mix in a stewpan with an ounce of butter, a little cream, pepper, salt, and sugar. Have ready some boiled vegetables, (peas, asparagus, or French beans, chopped not very small,) some chopped parsley and herbs, and stir these in with the eggs. A tarragon leaf, or small shalot, some fennel, a truffle or a little celery may be substituted when convenient. The whole should be served on hot toast.

CIII.—Egg Patties.

Make your usual patty paste, and shape. Mix a spoonful of butter, one of chopped spring onions, one of fried bread crumbs, some chopped parsley, salt and pepper, and put a layer in the bottom of each patty. Break an egg carefully into each ; put a very little Chili vinegar and parsley on the top of each egg, and cook gently in the oven; a slow fire will do best.

CIV.—Milanese Eggs.

Put 2 oz. of grated Parmesan into a stewpan with 1 oz. of butter, some parsley, two small onions chopped fine, and a tablespoonful of white wine (kitchen sherry will do). Stir over the fire till it is well mixed. Then break six eggs into a basin, put them into the stewpan, stir, and cook over a slow fire. Serve on slices of hot toast or fried bread.

CV.—Parma Eggs.

Put two yolks of eggs, a small pat of butter, and a tablespoonful of grated Parmesan cheese, with spice (nutmeg, mace, &c.,) into a flat dish, and stir on the hot plate. Break five or six eggs into it, and cover lightly with grated cheese. Brown it over, and serve.

CVI.—Golden Eggs.

Hard-boil the eggs, shell, and sprinkle them with flour. Beat up one or more raw eggs, and dip the hard eggs in this ; roll them in bread crumbs, and fry of a good golden brown. Serve in mushroom, Bechamel, or maitre d'hotel sauce.

CVII.—Eggs à la Pelle.

Boil the eggs nearly hard, put them into cold water, shell, and slice them, putting a little butter and chopped parsley between each slice. Have some very hot toast ready, lightly buttered; put the egg on this. Have ready mixed some chopped mushroom, (or gherkin, or onion,) butter, crumbs, seasoned with pepper and salt, and softened with a little cream. Spread over the eggs, and brown the whole with a salamander or shovel.

CVIII.—Buttered Eggs.

Put 2 oz. of butter with a little water into a stew-pan. Break six eggs into a basin, and stir them well; then pour into the pan, and stir till all is quite mixed. Then serve on hot buttered toast.

CIX.—Salisbury Buttered Eggs.

Hard boil and chop the eggs, put into a stewpan with butter, and season with pepper; mix well with a raw egg to blend. Serve on hot toast, and brown over with crumbs.

CX.—Provence Buttered Eggs.

Prepare the buttered egg as above, and before taking out of the saucepan stir in a spoon-ful of chopped mushroom, or parsley, or fresh boiled peas, or chopped gherkin according to the season.

CXI.—Eggs à la Soyer.

Boil the eggs hard, throw them into cold water, and take off the shells; then cut them into slices, put them into a saucepan with slices of onion about the same size, only thinner, which have been already boiled in milk. Add a little Bechamel sauce, a taste of garlic, a little pepper, nutmeg, and lemon juice. Toss well together over the fire, and when the eggs are hot serve with fried croutons.

CXII.--Curried Eggs.

Hard-boil the eggs, say six, and peel. Slice two onions, and fry them in oil or butter ; add a table-spoonful of curry powder, mix with a cupful of cream and a little flour to thicken. Let this simmer till quite smooth, and then pour it round the eggs, which may stand in the dish, their ends being cut.

CXIII.—Russian Curried Eggs.

The same, except that the hard eggs are to be sliced up, the curry sauce poured over them, and the whole garnished with very thinly sliced gherkin and sardine alternately.

CXIV.—Curried Vegetables.

Two ounces of butter, a tablespoonful of curry powder, a cupful of water with a little vinegar. Roll any vegetables in flour, aud stew in the above; stir in a little mashed potato mixed with curry powder, and stew till soft and quite hot.

CXV.--Onions en Matelote.

Put some large onions into boiling water for a minute ; drain and place them in a stewpan with salt, pepper, and a bunch of herbs. Brown them with some butter, throw in a chopped onion, and stir in a glass of common red wine and the yolk of an egg. Stew over a slow fire, and when served pour a little hot vinegar with some chopped gherkin over the onions. They should be served on fried croutons.

CXVI.—Onions au Riz.

Put four onions into a frying pan with butter enough to fry ; when getting brown, shake in three tablespoonfuls of rice (boiled and very dry, each grain separate). Add pepper, salt, a little mace, one or two cloves, a teaspoonful of sugar and another of vinegar, plain, Chili or Taragon. Shake up well and serve very hot.

CXVII.—Haricots à la Provencale.

Having thoroughly boiled the haricot beans, (in Provence green and white beans not dried are used together; if dry of course they must be soaked, as in No. 122) put them into a stewpan with several spoonfuls of olive oil, a couple of anchovies, some shalots, and a head of garlic bruised ; season with chopped parsley and gherkins, peppercorns, and salt. Fry them a few minutes, and dish ; add to what remains in the stewpan a little vinegar, boil, and pour over the beans.

CXVIII.—French beans à la Lyonnaise.

Wash, split, and blanch in boiling water ; then put into cold water and drain. Slice some onions, and redden them in butter in a frying pan ; then throw in the beans, and fry with chopped parsley, silver onions, salt and coarse pepper. Dish, pour some boiling vinegar over the beans, and serve.

CIX.—Spinage au Beurre.

Pick, wash several times, and drain well ; then throw the spinage into a saucepan of hot water with some salt, and boil till quite tender. Drain and squeeze out all the water ; then rub through a coarse wire sieve, and put into a stewpan with enough butter to moisten it thoroughly, salt and a little nutmeg. Stir with a wooden spoon ; when hot add a spoonful of any sauce and some more butter. Stir up well, and serve with fried croutons.

CXX.—Spinage à la Creme.

Proceed in the same way till it is hot, then stir in a gill of cream, with a pat of butter, and a large spoonful of pounded sugar, and stir well over the fire.

CXXI.—Spinage à l'Italienne.

Pick, wash, put into boiling water, drain, and squeeze. Then chop very fine, and stew in a saucepan with butter. Add while stewing a few sweet almonds pounded, with a bit of candied citron, chopped fine, a spoonful of powdered sugar, some salt, and nutmeg. Stir in a couple of eggs and a little cream. Mix well, and keep turning over the fire with a wooden spoon till quite thick. Pour out upon a dish sprinkled with flour, and let it get cold; cut into squares or ovals and fry lightly, sprinkle with sugar, and pass a hot iron over.

Sometimes this dish is eaten hot when first poured out, without being fried.

CXXII.—White Haricot Beans à la Francaise.

Steep the dried beans in cold water for some hours, (five or six at least,) and boil in cold water. Put the beans in a stewpan with two ounces of butter, salt and pepper, a spoonful of lemon juice, and chopped parsley. Mix well and serve.

CXXIII.—Potato Croquets.

Bake the potatoes, and rub through a sieve. Add to six potatoes one ounce of butter, three yolks of egg, and seasoning. Stir over the fire till quite mixed. When cold shape into balls, dip them into egg, roll in bread crumbs, and fry.

CXXIV.—Fried Potatoes.

Slice raw potatoes very thin, and throw them into cold water. Drain and dry them thoroughly on a cloth, and then fry quickly of a light brown. They should be quite dry and crisp.

CXXV.—Choux farcies.

Pass the cabbage in butter without letting it brown, and add some chopped mushrooms and parsley, a large spoonful of semolina, pepper, salt, and nutmeg. Take off the finest leaves of the cabbage, and cut the others two or three times across. Put them into boiling water, and drain. Then put some of the mixture between every leaf, and roll them up in the large outer leaves. Smear these with the mixture, and stew in a saucepan with a little water, butter, and a bunch of herbs.

CXXVI.—Potato Pudding.
(Swiss recipe.)

Two pounds of potatoes, boiled, and passed through a sieve. Add a quarter of a pound melted butter, and the ·same of powdered sugar. Mix well, and add six eggs thoroughly beaten as for an omelette, a glass of brandy, and a quarter of a pound of currants. Mix again thoroughly; put into a cloth, and tie it up carefully. Boil for half an hour, and serve in any sweet sauce, or with powdered sugar only.

CXXVII.—Potatoes à la Lyonnaise.

Take any remains of cold potatoes, shred them into a frying-pan containing three ounces of butter, and three sliced onions. Fry the potatoes brown.

Then add a large spoonful of boiled rice (very dry), parsley, pepper, salt, and some lemon juice, mix, fry altogether, and serve.

CXXVIII.—Potatoes à la Maître d'Hotel.

Slice boiled potatoes, and put the slices into a stewpan, with a little white sauce or maigre stock, two ounces of butter, chopped parsley, pepper and salt, and a spoonful of lemon juice. Toss until well mixed, and serve.

Or make the maître d'hotel sauce, and pour it very hot on the potatoes, arranged in circles on the dish.

CXXIX.—Potatoes en brun.

Cut up the potatoes (already boiled,) and fry them to a light brown; then sprinkle thickly with chopped parsley and shalot (or mushroom), pepper and salt, and lemon juice, and serve very hot.

CXXX.—Tomatas au Gratin.

Cut off the bottom of the tomatas, and take out the seeds carefully; put them into oil. Chop up one or two mushrooms and shalots, with some

E

parsley and thyme. Season with pepper and salt ; fry the whole for a few minutes, then add two yolks of egg, mix, and fill the tomatas. Sprinkle the surface with bread crumbs, and brown before serving.

CXXXI.—Cauliflower au gratin.

Wash the cauliflowers in hot water, with a little butter and salt, boil, and drain them well ; if large divide them. When dished pour over the following mixture, made meanwhile.

To a tablespoonful of white sauce add three ounces of grated cheese, one ounce and a half of butter, three yolks of egg, a teaspoonful of lemon juice, pepper, salt, and nutmeg, and stir in a saucepan, without quite boiling. Smooth this sauce over the cauliflower, and sprinkle the top with bread crumbs and grated cheese, and put in the oven for a quarter of an hour, when the crumbs should be well browned.

CXXXII.—Potatoes au gratin.

Slice boiled potatoes, and put a layer in a dish ; spread a layer of the same sauce as above over it ; then another (or more) layer of potatoes, each covered with the sauce. Sprinkle with bread crumbs and grated cheese, and put into the oven for about twenty minutes.

CXXXIII.—French Beans à la Maître d'Hotel.

Pick and cut into strips, wash and drain. Then throw the beans into boiling water with a good deal of salt, and boil quickly till they are tender ; then drain. Make your sauce ready in a stewpan : a spoonful of white sauce (or cream), two ounces of butter, a large tablespoonful of chopped parsley (partly boiled), nutmeg, pepper and salt, and a spoonful of lemon juice. Stir well, and when quite mixed throw in the beans and shake well together, serving very hot with fried croutons.

CXXXIV.—French Beans de Dijon.

Prepare as above. Put two ounces of butter with chopped parsley, two chopped shalots, some chopped thyme, and the heart of a lettuce also chopped, with pepper, salt, and nutmeg, and a large spoonful of lemon juice, into a saucepan ; simmer well, and throw the beans in as above.

CXXXV.—Potatoes à la Pelérine.

Slice some onions, and brown them in butter. Mix some boiled potatoes cut in rounds. Moisten the whole with milk, not *soaking* it ; sprinkle lightly with powdered sugar, boil for five or six minutes, and serve very hot.

CXXXVI.—Stewed Peas.

To a quart of peas, put one ounce of butter in cold water ; rub the peas and butter with your hand till they are mixed. Pour off the water, and put the peas in a stewpan with two lettuces cut up, some green onions, and parsley, a little salt, and a dessert-spoonful of powdered sugar. Let them stew for half-an-hour. Knead two ounces of butter in a plate, with a dessert-spoonful of flour ; mix with the peas, and toss well over the fire.

CXXXVII.—Petitspois au Sucre.

May be done in the same way, leaving out the lettuce, adding a spoonful of cream, and twice the quantity of sugar.

CXXXVIII.—Stewed Lettuce.

Boil two lettuces with salt till quite tender, then

put them in cold water. Cut them up, not very small, and put into a stewpan, with two tablespoonfuls of cream, a bit of butter, a teaspoonful of flour, pepper and salt. Some people add a sardine when serving.

CXXXIX.—Artichokes à la Reynière.

Cut some onions in small dice, pass them in butter till they are of a good brown colour, with pepper and salt : take them out of the stewpan, and let them get cold in the butter. Take off the leaves and choke of the artichokes, pare the bottoms, wash and drain them ; then fill them with the chopped onion, and sprinkle them with grated cheese and bread crumbs. Brown in the oven and serve.

CXL.—Celery in frittura.

Clean and trim the heads of celery, parboil them for ten minutes, and then put into cold water. Drain, and then stew gently till quite cooked. Let them get cold, and then throw the pieces into batter, and fry.

Or roll them in bread crumbs, and then dip in egg, and bread-crumb the outside.

CXLI.—Salsify in frittura.

Scrape the salsify till it is quite white; put it into cold water with a little vinegar, pepper and salt, and a bit of butter. Drain in a sieve; then put the pieces, about three inches long each, into two tablespoonfuls of oil, and one of vinegar, with pepper and salt. Steep them till nearly wanted, then drain them, and fry quickly in batter.

The same proceeding may be used as far as the oil, and then the salsify may be put into a stewpan with a little white sauce (or cream), adding a spoonful of lemon juice, a bit of butter, and some pepper. Serve up with fried bread.

CXLII.—Fried Jerusalem Artichokes.

Peel, cut them through lengthwise; salt them, drain; then sprinkle with flour, and fry either in oil, or in batter.

CXLIII.—Sweet Fritters of Celery.

Take the upper parts of the stalk, wash and blanch them in boiling water; then put into cold, drain, tie in a bundle, and boil thoroughly. Let them get cold, and when wanted sprinkle them with brandy (or other liqueur), powder with sugar, fry in batter, and serve with powered sugar.

CXLIV.—Jerusalem Artichokes, or Cardons, au Parmesan.

The vegetables should be prepared, as in the last recipe, and stewed in a maigre sauce. When dished, cover with grated Parmesan cheese and fine bread crumbs. Brown with the shovel, and serve.

CXLV.—Artichokes a la Provencale.

Pluck off all the coarse leaves (the artichokes should be tender,) and cut away the bottoms, snipping off the hard part of the leaves left ; pull these out as much as you can without removing them. Salt and pepper the inside, and pour olive oil in freely. Then put the artichokes separately into a stewpan, pouring oil in up to their chokes ; add a few sprigs of parsley and thyme. Cover the stewpan with a dish or soup-plate of water. The artichokes should stew thus for two hours over a slow fire, and be served in their own sauce.

CXLVI.—Calecannon.

Mix cold mashed potatoes and boiled greens smoothly; add a little butter, pepper and salt. Sprinkle with bread crumbs, brown, and serve very hot.

CXLVII.—Carrots à la Ménagère.

Cut the carrots in rounds, stew them in half maigre stock and half white wine, with salt, pepper, and herbs. When cooked, add some flour rubbed into butter. Let the whole boil a moment, and serve as hot as possible.

CXLVIII.—Carrots à l'Allemande.

Take a bunch of quite young carrots, parboil them with a little salt, drain ; then put into a stew-pan, with two ounces of butter, white sugar, and a pint of milk. Let them boil very gently, and serve in their own sauce, sprinkled with chopped parsley.

CXLIX.—Carrots à la Lungern.

Cut the carrots in rounds, stew them in any white sauce, with salt and a few herbs. While stewing sprinkle in a handful of green peas. Serve, adding a little white sauce before dishing, if necessary, and at the last moment stew a few very crisp dice of fried bread over the dish.

CL.—Stewed Mushrooms.

Take a handful of small round mushrooms, wash two or three times in cold water, pass them in a stewpan with fresh butter; add a few pinches of flour, a little salt and spice, and let them stew gently. When nearly done, add a little maigre stock, and let them simmer in a few minutes.

CLI.—Mushrooms au Gratin.

The large ones are best for this. Trim them, chop up two or three mushrooms, as much of shalot, and several sprigs of parsley. Put into a saucepan with butter, chopped thyme, and seasoning; fry for five minutes, then add two yolks of egg. Mix, and put the mixture into the mushrooms, sprinkle with bread crumbs, and bake in the oven for a quarter of an hour.

CLII.—Broiled Mushrooms.

The larger sized mushrooms are best for broiling, and those with rather curled edges. Having taken

off the stalks, put them on the gridiron upon a
sheet of oiled paper, and cover the inside edges
with olive oil, and minced parsley (and garlic),
sprinkling with pepper and salt. You must mind to
keep the oil evenly supplied while the mushrooms
are broiling ; but they should be served nearly dry.

Oil is better than butter for this purpose, but
either will do.

CLIII.—Mushrooms Sautés.

Clean and wash the mushrooms in vinegar and
water. Drain in a cloth ; sprinkle with salt, and
dredge with flour ; pass them in beaten egg, and
then in bread crumbs. Then put them in a stewpan with Bechamel sauce, seasoned with chopped
fennel, sprinkle a little fine bread crumb, and fry
with butter till of a good colour.

CLIV.—Minced Mushrooms.

Cut up the mushrooms in slices, blanch them in
vinegar and water with a little salt, drain and dry
them in a cloth ; then fry quickly in butter,
sprinkling with pepper and salt, and throw them
into a Maître d'Hôtel Sauce.

CLV.—Œufs à la Tomata.

Hard boil and shell the eggs, cut them in two lengthwise; cut up the whites in strips, and heat them in tomata sauce. Put this on a dish, within a circle of fried croutons; grate the yolks over it and alternate once or twice thus, ending with the grated yolks. Bake and serve.

CLVI.—Mushrooms à la Fermière.

Take two good sized mushrooms, and stew them. Meanwhile chop up another mushroom with a hard boiled egg, a spoonful of cream and a little pepper. Put this into the centre of the mushrooms while stewing, with a tiny bit of butter on the top, and serve on toast very hot.

CLVII.—Potato Hash.

One pound of potatoes, one onion chopped fine, chopped parsley and herbs, a little bit of butter, the pounded yolks of two eggs, pepper, salt, spice, and a little sugar. Stew, moistening with milk from time to time, and serve very hot, sprinkled with bread crumbs browned.

CLVIII.—The same au Fromage.

The only difference is that before serving you should sprinkle a little grated cheese instead of bread crumbs, and brown it with a salamander.

CLIX.—Ragout de Béarne.

The same as (No. 157) only using turnips instead of potato, and putting on the bread crumbs rather thickly, some bits of butter among them, before browning.

CLX.—Potato Pie.

Take some cabbage that has been dressed before, and one or two carrots ; put with a little butter, pepper, and salt in the bottom of a dish. Then put a thick layer of raw potatoes thinly sliced; sprinkle with pepper, a little flour, and a teaspoonful of vinegar. Put this into the oven till the potatoes are thoroughly cooked, and before serving cover with a pie crust of mashed potato, allowing time for it to get well browned.

CLXI.—St. Quentin Potato Pie.

Slice the potatoes thin ; lay among the slices some chopped onion, and some shredded mushrooms. Sprinkle with pepper, salt, and flour, and add a few little bits of butter; moisten with some water or Maigre Stock, and a tablespoonful of milk or cream (or olive oil) with as much mustard powder as it will take up. Then cover with a very light puff paste, and bake.

CLXII.—Potatoes à la Bonnefemme.

Slice some cooked potatoes and carrots; lay them in alternate rings (not over but inside one another). Put some fried croutons round them, and pour a very hot Bechamel or other white sauce over them, and serve.

CLXIII.—Potato Soufflé.

Bake six large potatoes for an hour. Scoop out the inside thoroughly, taking care not to break the skins. Rub the pulp through a wire sieve. Boil a little milk, and put the potato, with one yolk of egg, pepper and salt, in; whip all together. Then fill up the potato skins with the mixture, bake quickly, till the pulp rises out of the top, and serve.

CLXIV.—Bread Cutlets.

Cut some stale bread into cutlet shapes; soak

these for three hours in new milk, drain, and fry in clarified butter till very crisp. Serve up either with pepper and salt, and one of the above savoury sauces, or with wine sauce and jam.

CLXV.—Maigre Rissolles.

With half a pound of boiled rice take three raw yolks of egg, two spoonfuls of cream, pepper and salt ; stir over the fire. When cold, take a table-spoonful, and in the midst put a tiny bit of butter, and a peppercorn. Roll up into a ball, egg, and bread crumb, and fry light brown. Serve with fried parsley.

CLXVI.—Macaroni Rissolles.

The same, substituting well boiled macaroni, cut into quite short pieces, for the rice.

CLXVII.—Potato Rissolles.

Take some very smooth, cold mashed potato in the same way ; put a bit of butter and a small bit of gherkin into the centre. Roll into balls, and fry as before.

CLXVIII.—Macaroni à la Suisse.

Boil two ounces of macaroni, and drain. Mix

two tablespoonfuls of flour, and a few peppercorns, in two tablespoonfuls of water; pour half-a-pint of boiling milk over this, and stir well. Then add the macaroni with four well-beaten eggs. Stir, seasoning with sugar, salt, nutmeg, a bit of bay leaf, and a little cinnamon, and brown in the oven. Some people serve sardines with this dish.

CLXIX.—Macaroni.

Two ounces of macaroni put into hot water; let it simmer with a little salt till quite tender. Strain, and put into a stewpan, with a little plain white sauce. Serve very hot, with or without fried bread crumbs sprinkled over it.

CLXX.—Cheese Macaroni.

Boil half-a-pound of macaroni; then put into a a stewpan with two ounces of butter, two ounces of grated cheese, and a tablespoonful of cream; add pepper and salt, and mix well over the fire till quite hot. Shake it up, and brown the top before serving.

CLXXI.—Macaroni Fritters.

Make a paste of boiled macaroni cut small, with

grated cheese, and a little cream, pepper and salt ; (the macaroni should be partly in small pieces still.) Then sprinkle with grated cheese, make into little irregular pieces, and fry in batter.

CLXXII.—Savoury Rice Pudding.

Wash a teacupful of rice, and boil it with three large onions, a mealy potato, an egg, four ounces of butter, a little chopped celery and herbs, pepper, salt, and sugar. It should boil for nearly two hours.

The same may be varied by adding a little chopped pickle of any kind.

CLXXIII.—Fried Rice.

Boil a cupful of rice, drain ; then fry it with a little butter, sprinkling in a very little cayenne and saffron powder, salt, and sugar. Some people add a few raisins.

CLXXIV.—Parmese Rice.

Fry a sliced onion in oil or butter, with a few (shelled) shrimps, prawns, or bits of lobster, stirring in a dessertspoonful of mustard. When hot, put in a cupful of boiled rice (very dry), and a table-spoonful of Parmesan cheese. Stir, and serve very hot.

CLXXV.—Vegetable Pudding.

Take spinage, peas, and broad beans, boiled each separately, and rubbed through a sieve. Mix with the whites of two eggs, a little pepper and salt ; fill a basin, and boil.

CLXXVI.—Curry Salad.

Slice boiled potatoes and Portugal onions (the latter cold), place in a dish, and pour curry sauce very hot over them.

CLXXVII.—Curry Custard.

Break three or four eggs into a basin, and beat them up, add a quart of milk, a little salt and sugar, and two teaspoonfuls of curry powder; bake in a mould, and serve.

CLXXVIII.—Curried Macaroni.

Boil the macaroni till tender, dish, and pour the curry sauce (No. 32) over it.

F

CLXXIX.—Curried Potatoes.

Slice boiled potatoes hot, and pour the same curry over them.

CLXXX.—Curried Fish.

Half boil the fish, cut it up and put it into a stewpan with butter, chopped onion, and pepper. Stew till the fish is soft, then add a spoonful of curry powder, stew a little longer, dish, and serve with very dry boiled rice on a separate dish.

CLXXXI.—Curried Eggs.

Hard boil the eggs, cut one end so that they will stand upright, and serve in the curry sauce.

CLXXXII.—Curry Toast.

Make a thick paste of curry powder with chilli vinegar. When it is of a consistence just to drop from the spoon beat it up well with a little pounded fish of any kind, or with the hard yolks of two eggs. Moisten with a little cream, make very hot in a stewpan, and serve on hot buttered toast.

CLXXXIII.—Toast au Diablerets.

Make some French mustard into a paste with

chili vinegar. Spread any pounded fish on a slice of hot toast, cover with the paste, put on a thinner piece of hot toast and serve.

The same may be done without fish, buttering the toast, then spreading the mustard paste, sprinkling with bread crumbs, adding some very thin slices of pickle and covering with hot toast.

CLXXXIV.—Anchovy Toast.

Bone and wash three or four Anchovies, pound them with a little butter, mixing in a small teaspoonful of mustard, some peppercorns and a few drops of chili vinegar. Have your slices of toast buttered hot, or fry some bread ready, and spread the paste on and serve very hot.

CLXXXV.—Indian Toast.

Take the remains of any cooked fish, (sole or haddock especially), chop and pound with a little butter, mixing in a teaspoonful of curry powder, a teaspoonful of French mustard, and moistening the paste sufficiently with chili vinegar. Spread on hot toast of fried bread as above.

CLXXXVI.—Anchovy Butter.

Clean half a dozen anchovies, pound them in a mortar with two ounces of butter, a little cayenne pepper and nutmeg, and a dessertspoonful of anchovy paste. Rub through a wire sieve. This is useful for Anchovy toast, Scotch woodcock, &c.

CLXXXVII.—Indian Butter.

Take a basinful of herbs—tarragon, parsley, chives, thyme, &c., parboil them and drain in a cloth. Add six anchovies, a spoonful of capers, a tablespoonful of curry powder, a little cayenne, and four ounces of butter. Pound altogether and rub through a wire sieve.

CLXXXVIII.—Viennese Salad.

Boil one or two large Portugal onions, and beet-root (separately). When cold cut into slices, and place alternately in any salad sauce, vinegar and oil, cream, or mustard and tarragon vinegar.

CLXXXIX.—Russian Salad.

Is made with cooked beetroot, carrot, and parsnip in slices, with chopped gherkins and capers, and a sharp vinegar sauce.

CLXC.—Dutch Salad.

Beetroot, potatoes, sliced apple, and celery. Add oil and vinegar, pepper and salt, and if you please, a little chopped anchovy, herring, or other salt fish.

CLXCI.—Galette Cake

One pound fine flour. Put it in a heap on the table, make a hole in the midst, and put in a large spoonful of salt and the same of sugar ; half a pound of butter, and a cupful of water, and knead all together. When the flour and butter begin to mix well, sprinkle in some more water, kneading all the time with the other hand. Work the paste well, spreading it on the table with the heavy part of the hand, and when it is quite smooth make it into a ball, and leave it for half an hour. Then roll it out two or three or four inches thick, cut the edges, and space it out, cutting in about an inch ; turn it, put on a baking tray, glaze with the yolk of egg whipped, put the tray on a hotplate and bake. It ought to take about half an hour.

CLXCII.—Potato Hot Cakes.

Take some very light mashed potato, knead

with flour, moistening with a little milk ; add salt.
Roll out to about a quarter of an inch thick, and
bake on a griddle.   Serve very hot for breakfast or
tea.

CLXCIII.—German Gauffres.

A quarter of a pound of sugar to two eggs, mix
with a quarter of a pound of flour, and half that
quantity of melted butter, and a little water and
some salt.   Mix well, divide, and bake.

CLXCIV.—Carlsbad Gauffres.

Drop a small tumbler full of flour into the same of
skim-milk, add an egg.   Beat up with three table
spoonfuls of sugar, a little salt, and bake.

Printed by A. R. Mowbray & Co., Oxford.